Divine Margins

BOOKS BY PETER COOLEY

The Company of Strangers (1975)
The Room Where Summer Ends (1979)
Nightseasons (1983)
The Van Gogh Notebook (1987)
The Astonished Hours (1992)
Sacred Conversations (1998)
A Place Made of Starlight (2003)
Divine Margins (2009)

DIVINE MARGINS

Poems by Peter Cooley

Carnegie Mellon University Press
Pittsburgh 2009

ACKNOWLEDGMENTS

Thanks are due to the editors of the following magazines in which these works or versions of these works first appeared:

AGNI Online: "Talk to the Dead"
Alaska Quarterly Review: "Writing Toward the Resurrection of Christ's Body at the Beginning of the Third Millennium," "Naming-the-Animals-Moments"
Commonweal: "The Rapture"
Epoch: "Introduction to Art History"
Hotel Amerika: "Emmaus Mornings"
Literary Imagination: "To the Morning Trees"
Margie: "Proem," "Proem Two: Almost Posthumous Poem," "Proem Three: All My Poems Are Aubades"
New England Review: "Television"
North American Review: "Born Blind"
Pleiades: "The Annunciation," "The Leaves; The Animals; The Sky Unseen," "The One Certain Thing"
Poetry East: "The Place of an Aubade"
The Second Wellington, New Zealand International Poetry Festival Anthology: "To My Mother and Father"
The Southern California Anthology: "Azaleas"
The Southern Review: "Release, Release," " First Light Meditation"
Volt: "All My Tests Negative"
"Naming-the-Animals-Moments" was cited in *Notable Essays of 2003* (selected by Robert Atwan) in *The Best American Essays 2004*, Louis Menard and Robert Atwan, editors. "Born Blind" was cited for special mention in 2005 *Pushcart Prize XXIX, Best of the Small Presses*, edited by Bill Henderson. "Emmaus Mornings" appeared in *Poetry Calendar 2006* (selected by Shafiq Naz).

Special thanks are due to Michael Kuczynski, Elizabeth Thomas, Kay Murphy, Carolyn Hembre, Andy Young, Ed Skoog, Brad Richard, Major Jackson, Jacki Cooley, Nicole Cooley, Alissa Cooley Rowan and Josh Cooley for their invaluable assistance.

Book design by Caitlinn Cork

The publication of this book is made possible by a grant from the Pennsylvania Council on the Arts.

PENNSYLVANIA
COUNCIL
ON THE
ARTS

Library of Congress Control Number 2008923984
ISBN 978-0-88748-494-0
Printed and bound in the United States of America

10 9 8 7 6 5 4 3 2 1

CONTENTS

To the memory of my parents

ONE

"Man has places in his heart which do not yet exist, and into them enters suffering, in order that they may have existence."
—Léon Bloy

TELEVISION

Because we knew we were nearing the end
of our long term together, my parents and I,
this last year of their moment on earth,
watched television all day, drawing us closer.

It was our campfire when I visited.
Morning: the news of last night's murders in Detroit.
Noon: the latest on the morning's death count.
Evening: after 4:30 dinner, more bodies piling up.

Of course, I was bored. Boredom was a balm
to watching them descend the long hill I'm still climbing.
We talked about my son, 16: his car scoping out heights of the night.
Because he was theirs they loved him—the comfort of lineage.

And after they both died, while I cleaned the apartment,
I kept the television on without ceasing.
I prayed the kaleidoscope of color would bring back
that ravening, the hollow in my chest

I grew up with, always starved for more from them.
Dying betrayed that hunger, leaving me everything
in trust. Television worked: clamor and flash,
childhood in fast-forward, not the numb question of
   immortality.

TRIPTYCH: CENTER PANEL ALWAYS STILL UNFINISHED

I: In Search of an Aubade

Mornings I had awakened to live forever
in the sequestering dark, calling the first birds
I told myself until then I knew how to answer
in music across this page—Who-Bird, What-Bird—
your voice did not resound there, Mother.
Now, three months dead, you are everywhere I turn.
And today I know my time here is momentary,
What-Bird, Why-Bird, Name-Bird, drawing them all to you,
I am the smallest of the small: the day is all
dapples and shadows as the light falls and rises,
every bird retreating with glare of a full sun.
Mother, your voice: there is no word for how it wounds me.
It comes back as that silence you picked up the phone with
            always,
hesitant, plangent, dawn lifting back the night.
Mother, your voice, I only have it at first light.

II: Epithalamium: The Night of My Mother's Death

My parents' marriage: ended after seventy years,
still impenetrable as mine at half that time.
Mother dead seven hours, my father busy
at the business of grief, I try here to rob a grave
husband and wife lie down in with the years
neatly stacked above them.
                        What would my wife never answer,
Mother, if she were to come back, hair dripping
wild from the other world? What, Mother?
Separations, joinings, the cemetery of errors
we are still compiling, understandings scant?
Weigh in, too, hours of undertakings, each assembled

to make sure the other feels mired in separation
from that soul's companion we'd sworn to comfort, honor, keep,
in sickness and in health until death do us etc.

Oh, they don't come back, except in the old poetries!

Who can understand the secrets of another's bedroom?
My parents' marriage: they stayed married the duration.

III: Call and Response

Now, six months into your afterlife,
you have begun to speak to me.
What I wanted would have been the world
come back rapturous, clear as the first day
I knew I was Peter. You lift me up,
the bars gnarling around my little sleep.
You call that word, your cheek nuzzling, cool
pressed to my flaming cheek. Down the years: *Peter*.
But, no, your return has been your own,
fifteen minutes each day. I am counting out the seconds.

Today you assure me you heard me, flying in
to speak across the broken, morphined sleep
you woke from moments. So I was not too late?
I held your hand. What could be said I said.

Mother, you repeat this every morning, leaving:
together we'll travel back as the years pass
until in our memory we're one body, finally.

THE RAPTURE

Beyond the window he stares out, oblivious
I've come back, my father is entering the afterworld.
I am still here, working Dad's "senior residence,"
occasional nurse, valet, waiter and errand boy,
a pint of cherry ice cream leaking a slow drip in my hand.

Out there, they are together in a first snow,
my father and mother, she nine months dead,
two tiny figures walking backward to Paradise.
This is before my sister and her madness, the war,
before I appear, then relatives demanding bed and board for
        years.
Snow dots his top hat; it mists her wedding veil.
Snow is all they know, and darkness for the blizzards
to fall across these decades they walk away from now.

Soon in their backward amble they will enter
the gates, swung open for them, and begin to shed their clothes,
flinging everything skyward as their new bodies come together.

LITTLE QUARTET FOR MY FATHER

I

Toward the end, which, I see now, I was blind to,
my father, who dressed for dinner at the home
as Mother had, he in his matching blues for coat and tie,
pleaded one morning to stay in pajamas all day long.
Almost to the hour Mother had been dead nine months.
He begged me, too, to clean out his closet,
give the Salvation Army Brooks Brothers suits,
ties from London and Paris and Madrid.
Shamed into his suit, I wheeled him, unwilling, to dinner.
The next night he lost all appetite. Propped up in navy blue,
he spooned down a cup of consommé to please me.
On Christmas Eve he threw his bowels up, they said.
They said he was splattered with black shit when he stopped
          breathing.

II

Roast beef, gray meat, bun stuck
to plastic enshrouding it: I stuff half in,
eyeing my seat partner's airline dinner,
stuff the second half so fast she asks me
would I like hers. I wash that down
with apple juice, fall instantly asleep.
When I awake, we are landing in your death.

III

Last things, lost things, is there a difference?
Dawn finds me riffling through my father's last stuff
before the junkman comes. What did Dad think
his last night, Christmas Eve, hospital after hospital

too booked to take him in? Last place, lost place,
St. Mary's, where he lay for hours
waiting for a room. Last room, last conversation,
lost conversation, the one we never had
that night or our whole lives, I'm calling to you now,
Dad, too late, café au lait, I think I'll have one later,
it's only in B-movies or in Dickens,
the deathbed scene ties up some Windsor knot
like the one you taught me, to teach my son.
Last conversation. Fathers teach us to be men,
Dad, you did fine. Final, finitude. I think I'll throw out the tie
      rack.
I'm glad I'm talking to you now, Dad, right here.
Tell me later what you think? The junk guy's knocking to get in.

IV

After my father died, desire died in me.
My body walked beside me, a companion,
no, a shadow; no, a friend I had outgrown
and wished to consign to rooms of childhood,
both of us skidding our trucks across the floor.
My wife sleeping beside me—I could touch her,
taking in the scent of woman, that musk
enough to drive me wild years, oh, even last year!
and feel beneath my fingers her skin in a glass case.
I ran my fingers on my reflection there. He stared back,
      disappeared.
Women on the street; designs in a tableau;
circle, square, triangle, I took them in, no more to me
than offices I passed, crammed with others' swarming lives.
I was the glass man: light passed through me, light passed me by.

BLUE RING

All I have left of him that I can touch
I wear on my right hand's middle finger.
Not much to look at, is it? Watery blue
the stone, worth nothing so the jeweler said,
catching the day hard as I go through it
in light's huge imperfections, glittering,
mastering light, making light all its own.

Even as a kid he didn't touch me
nearly enough. Therefore, I touch my son,
eighteen, repeatedly at his shoulder
whenever I catch him on the run, rushed
to get out of here, onto his life
just as Dad was that last month in the home,
staring out after Mother died at clouds
re-shaping ugly Michigan winter.
Back to the ring. It didn't fit—
too big and no good way to cut it down
without breaking, the bored jeweler told me.
Your father's? Wear it as it is. No charge.
Someday you'll come back and purchase something.
But I have a ring to catch up the day
like a little boy with his magic toy.
I travel light and light is everything.
On my fist I wear his gift, blue-clenched,
reflecting heaven some days, some not.
He left me his imperfection to go on.

LITTLE QUARTET FOR MY MOTHER

I

Dying requires so little of ourselves.
Sitting beside my mother at the end
I watched the winter light late afternoon
preparing its descent. Cloud upon cloud,
Mother and I were together, birds mid-air,
riding these billows now within the room.
For an hour there was no difference between there and here.
And then Mother had to go. I let myself
disentangle from the terrible great shaking
she surrendered to while we re-entered this small room.
All my body ached, I wanted sleep. Mother was busy dying.
I knew we could never be this close ever again.
But when I heard her breathing slowing, slowly
I stood up. My warm palm touched my own wet forehead.
I'm tired of dying, I said. And then she was gone.

II

In her last year my mother, eyesight gone,
hearing quickly diminishing, would watch the light
she knew was acting out its daily life
beyond my father, perfect vision fixed on stock returns,
his chair until the end pressed to their one window.
When I entered, she would tell me she was taking in
noon sun she ran with during recess at country school,
or evening, shadows closing ranks around our first house in
      Detroit.
I remember her clutching a book, one of her favorites,
Dickens maybe, playacting like my daughter, who at two,
longing to imitate, told me she was reading.
But Mother's pages were the color of no color, she confessed,

like my face when I bent to kiss her each night, leaving.
That blind kiss stung my cheek, still hangs here, aching.

III

Touch me, I am alive, I wanted to shout
to shoppers cramming baskets with brown sugar, cream of
    wheat,
my mother's beginning to a day she shared with me at two,
the taste that sweetness of my first words someone heard.
She lifts the spoon into my mouth. . . . And now she's dead.
But I'm alive beside these bodies treading water in the aisles.
Readers, I'd have you all consumers of this fare.
Nothing else is here: brown sugar, cream of wheat,
and me again in the body I rose with
this morning to assume the day one week after her death.
Cream of wheat, brown sugar, I drop them in my cart,
no one but you knowing how little I've become,
readers, how little I need now since Mother's gone.
Breakfast at the beginning, supper for the end of life.

IV

Now the day my mother died I was occupied
with crying and not crying, digging in
to grieving. But, just one day after,
I awoke to the dead world. I saw springtime,
dogwood, my favorite harbinger, clusters of black buds
beside azaleas dappled with darkness
and the ground, high noon to evening, shadows only
I would have rushed to throw myself inside
had they been singular. I said: everything is dead.
Even you, Love, I saw your sleeping body

19

a corpse laid out and looked in on my son,
stirring in the stupor of sixteen, soon to burst forth
standing dead in the kitchen, demanding eggs and cereal.
A dead man walked in my steps, spoke his first words.
These words are the dead poem he-speaking-through-me said.

FIRST BIRTHDAY LETTER TO THE DEAD

Mother, today you would be ninety-five.
I celebrate your birthday with this poem.
Two years you have been "gone" and when Dad "went"
(these were the words the two of you would use
discussing death you knew was just ahead)
eleven months later, I knew you were dead
but writing this you're here, talking me through,
miraculous, isn't it, what poetry can do?
Question: Is there weather there? *Yes, of course.*
Food? *Naturally.* Books? *All the ones you know.*
The stuff you read me when I was little?
Every single page and new ones you've never seen.
Who's there? How's Dad? What do you do all day?
You ask too many questions. I have to go.
We'll write a poem next year. You're still too young for more,
    you know.

SECOND BIRTHDAY LETTER TO THE DEAD

Dad, you would have been ninety-four today.
I celebrate by trying to bring your body back.
First, rising before dawn, your habit,
then scanning the stock page as if I were ten,
imitating you until at fourteen
I admitted all I liked was poetry there:
General Motors, General Foods, General Electric,
and turned from you to such hate and my words
as could help me stand alone. Today I stand
beneath the shower head, remembering
age three or so, I'm standing at your knee,
you toss me the soap, I drop it, transfixed,
thinking I'll never have one that big, that thick,
all rooted in black hair. And now I'm here,
you're there, my son at seventeen
too old for showers with me, hating me probably
in his own way. But we have your birthday,
don't we, to celebrate, to be a man
simplified around a few intentions like this poem,
most of them good, all of them decent.
Such mornings, clear skies, you have given me.

UNDERWEAR; MY CONCEPTION;
THE SALVATION ARMY

When someone dies, going through their underwear
(I mean "their," I did Mother's and then Dad's)
has to be done. Both times I put if off.
Both times it was bleak Michigan winter,
January, they died a year apart.
I chose the half hour just before dinner
at the nursing home where I took my meals
each death visit, eating with their neighbor,
who slept, his mouth open, all afternoon,
denying he ever slept. Just like my dad.
Here's how it went: my mother's underpanties,
my father's shorts, these they removed one night
sixty years back. Explosions high with stars?
I hope that they could come together, yes,
conceiving me, I hope they took their time,
that I was planned, to end up a fair man,
giving half the panties (how small they were,
how ragged the elastic, how frayed, torn,
my father's shorts he pulled his cock from
to pee every half hour at the end)
to The Salvation Army, half of Dad's shorts, too,
half to Goodwill, the third half just my past
I packed in plastic garbage bags to tote
downstairs where garbage men took them as I ate.

FOR MY DEAD FATHER ON FATHER'S DAY

If there is only the world, then these small words,
self-harrowing, dig their own hell on earth.
But if there is more than you-were-I-am,
well, then, huzzahs to the departed, Dad,
and, listen, what do you make of today in Paradise?
I'm running down my block to the Mississippi,
the filthy whore of Babylon
spread out, giving herself up to the sun.
Are you with me? Once I ran here with my son,
eighteen now, matured to other pleasures
and you are more my son than father here.
Dad, I'm holding your hand, kneel down with me,
lift up your palms, take in the stigmata,
imagination insists we are saints.
For the moment in my soul you are here, alive.

LETTERS FROM THE DEAD

I: From My Mother

You who have read as I read when I was eight
that the sea will disgorge at the end of time
its centuries of dead, walk with me now,
listen with me as a blue rain ticks down
from your roof. This is not Armageddon, just another day
I am out of life, a spirit, today age eight
and this same sun freckling the autumn grass
drew me out, another morning, summer ending,
1915 and after, seventy-five years
into a world I never learned to love enough.

Today, hand in hand, we will walk back
until I am that little girl, flowers in hand
she presses into a book, *A Child's Garden of Verses,*
cowslip, Queen Anne's lace, Wild Clover,
a piece of that day breaking off in my son's hand
today, June 9, 2007. Now I look down,
he is so small from here, my son at late middle-age.
I watch him press it to his nose, scentless,
his lips, to see him taste it, tasteless, kissing it.
And I would not come back, not even when he cries
and the memory of me flickers while he tries, failing at this.

II: From My Father

Morning begins: the world outside my window
waited for me while I slept: the blue so struck
with gold, as dawn arrives, it lifts me up.
I throw the covers back, already I am in the hour,
a boy come to Detroit from Flint to make his way
as my father never did or could. There never came a way.

Just work and work and then my wife, daughter, son,
a mother-in-law, sister-in-law, the cousins,
a house of others I had to feed and clothe.
But this morning I am seventeen, throwing off the dark
and no one in my father's house is up to shake off my dream.
I'll go out to the streetcar, then climb the office steps,
where I am youngest clerk, arriving early, leaving late,
a habit I will take on to become my life.
And the habit like the role of a priest at his last rite
will be the one I live by seventy years until the end.
And now in this place without night or morning,
light or dark, I am alone with it
in the absence of mourning, unemployed
or idle, all eternity a long hour I can't think how to fill.

THE PLACE OF AN AUBADE

Mornings, sometimes my body is my prayer
parting the air before me, right foot, left:
proceeding is enough—or tries to be—
that I get the fundamental out: sky, sun,
clouds, birds, trees, earth churning beneath my feet.
Now, Lord, You who appear if asked for
as I ask, now, this minute, help me to fit
my arms through sleeves, my legs down the loose pants,
the chain and mail the wind designed for me.
Ah, the sun fits exactly when I fit it on my head!
And the ground? No better cobbler than cement,
a new pair of shoes each time I take a step.
When I begin to run, I am one with You.
And then words You whisper to me,
I tell myself, immortal, are my poetry.

Two

"There is another world and it is in this one."
—Paul Eluard

WRITING TOWARD THE RESURRECTION OF CHRIST'S BODY AT THE BEGINNING OF THE THIRD MILLENNIUM

"Christ between His Parents Returning from the Temple" by Rembrandt

I

Thinking about Jesus always ends the same:
I shift between these poles just as He swings
in Rembrandt's etching, parents at either hand.
Joseph, as usual, dumbstruck, mystified,
leans on his walking stick, and Mary, staring
through Christ's upturned face, prepares herself
for His death with words He will impart to the doctors.

II

But when the dead come back they are old and cross.
My father stretches out, diapered in his bed.
He does not want changing. My mother cries.
She tells me she wants to die right now.
She keeps repeating she will not be x-rayed,
she has nothing more to say to me. In that dream I argue.
I argue too much when the dead come back, forgetting
it would be better to let them have their say,
their stay. After all, they have to be back,
wherever it is they came from, come morning.

III

I was a child until my parents died.
Fixed in that etching, I walked sixty years.
Last year, man at last, I saw my death
in theirs: it was nothing extraordinary.
In fact, both bodies delivered up to fire,
life appeared a flicker. I had to consider
words spoken by Rembrandt's figure, His short life—
about eternity, never worried on till now.

AMONG CLERKS AND CUSTOMERS

I

Soul workers, admit you have known God like me,
seen or unseen, His face never visible.
But in my dream, the temple split in two
top to bottom just as when Christ drew his last
and when I asked, or rather cried, so there is God,
a voice answered, "Yes," and from the crumbling wall
two woolly mammoths burst, tusks raised, heralding . . .

Great stuff, visions, dreams. Tonight my wife goes on
and on and on, as I am dropping off
because I didn't pay my speeding ticket on time
or fill up her car last night or rein in
my son, eighteen, from staying out too late.

II

Prompts Toward a Description of
Christ's Body on the Cross

Let it begin with my body in his waking,
waking to take in the world: the world has suffered while
          I slept,
slept that in another continent war rages,
rages that I get up, dressed in my pain,
pain in such countries never to be my own.
Owning of mine is a capitalistic venture,
venture I am free to start by walking,
walking alone down a quiet street,
street the birds are waking to, archangels, listen.
Listen, I am free to sing aloud, to lay my song by theirs.
There, I have released them, all the narratives of blue
blue moves to: my body aches, starting to run.

III

Soul worker, is it blue Monday for you, too?
This morning I saw God-the-visible
awakening in the face of that salesclerk
at the Quick Stop paying for gas at dawn.
She was surrounded by the lost, their beers,
snuff, lotto cards and in the parking lot, their crack.
We exchanged a smile, and then her cliché struck:
Have a blessed day. Yes, everything I turn to can be blessed.

DEATH OF THE AUTHOR

Marvelous that pool the lame man stared into,
more marvelous, deeper, ever more crystalline
each day another entered first. All hope
he had surrendered until Christ touched him:
Christ's touch, Christ's word, the text we read today.
But when I say "text" in my postmodern way,
reader, I being, as you know, quite dead
but resurrected within myself as I write,
I mean "text" as the blue sky and, yes, my car.
Stepping into it I'm in a chariot,
all four wheels fire. Come, slide in.
Fasten your seat belt. We'll paint the morning
any color as we ride, transforming
together, everything we look upon.
That dead tree? Singing, bird-filled as I speak.

INTRODUCTION TO ART HISTORY

What I like best about the Old Masters,
their aesthetic, which, in part, is responsible
for the long history of Western art
even after Descartes. They believe in beauty.
No, what I like best: their belief in Jesus.
Oh, Masters, take me back where I belong.
Today, Sunday, running in myself
though City Park, I saw the multitudes
and they were not as in Tintoretto's
"The Miracle of the Loaves and Fishes,"
arranged in silk, gold, brocade and such hues
as correspond nicely on the color wheel.
Motley, they barbecued: rich and poor,
black and white, they scattered trash over the grass.
A drunk fell from a tree, an ambulance was called.
I smelled pot and sweat, smoke, booze, the sun beat down.
There was no Christ at the center of the centerfold
of this art book. There was my life.
A friend waved me over. I was ravenous.
Crawfish étouffé, shrimp remoulade, French bread,
bread pudding with rum sauce.
I ate and ate and ate and ate till it was dark.

I: The Supper at Emmaus

Plenteous repasts here in Caravaggio,
tables laden with goodies to make us salivate,
a quail on silver platter, grapes and candied pears,
the flesh on one the same hue as Christ's face,
or on the travelers' hands, lifted in astonishment
so we follow the supernal while it manifests
shadow-light-shadow as our art teachers taught us—
how great it would have been to have this now today!

But I must content myself with miracles
such as become a life circumscribed like mine
I can pass on: look, these are my hands and feet.
The flesh before the mind is present in belief.
Pained they have been, they have had their pain lifted
that they become a second body, some new man.
All this came to me with my believing. Do you follow me?

II: Judas

Seldom seen at all in the Old Masters,
especially with Him, you are a word,
an old joke: who would give his son your name?
Were you intelligent, handsome, well-born?
Some of us would ask: did you have lots of women,
servants, houses, stuff which sets guys off
in each others' eyes and you surrendered quickly
to follow Him? Because in American society
a man does not touch, let alone kiss, men
except his father and then up to what, age ten?
It is the gesture of betrayal which fascinates me.
I hear the smack of your chosen perdition,
wondering why fame was so important to you
you'd choose it over my certain certainties,
a new car, flirtations with a waitress, immortality.

III: Christ in the Wilderness

Because imagination must begin
with the small, with facts, circumscribed in paint,
Christ's wilderness in the Old Masters
never exceeds the dimension of my yard.
Temptation doesn't need much playing room.

The devil's world is all about the little.
Look, I found a stone here in the grass.
It's dawn, I'm starving, but I'll leave it there.

When I stare beyond the trees, the infinite appears:
I don't have to work to take in the whole world,
Greece, Rome, our station on Mars, in a moment of time.
Next, I'm scaling the temple I erect here
this very second. And then dismantle it.
What a good exercise for morning, Christ—
an hour with You and the devil's gone for good.
Well, no. Just for today. Oh, probably till noon anyway.

FAILED SONNET

Just as Christ called Matthew and he followed,
leaving behind his business, receipt of custom,
so I walk out these mornings to attend the day
not yet risen, abandoning my wife and son asleep,
all the responsibility the day will ask
an hour from now. But for these minutes unaccountable
God walks with me, each step a grace note
in the score the street lays out. Holy the idiot mutt
barking at me though he knows me ten years now,
holy the mockingbird I pretend I've never heard before.
Oh, Lord, how ordinary Your revelation insists on staying
despite my efforts to dress You up in sonnet form.
No one is here but Petrarch, Shakespeare, Donne,
Yeats, their shades immortal, come out to promenade with me.
And yet I pride myself on keeping loneliness, yipping, nipping,
a shadow pooch, to tear along beside me.
He keeps my pace nice and crazy despite his familiarity.

ANOTHER OF MY POEMS ABOUT THE BODY

And then there is Christ's resurrected body—
reader, take, eat this poem given for you
that you may live eternally in my belief.
I claim that much for these lines if you will follow them.
Why should I claim less and write about myself,
my Midwestern adolescence, my mad sister,
my long surviving marriage?
My sparrows on the lawn are my sparrows.
Let's talk about our bodies, all the same
male or female, Death is working on.
Mine at late middle age has aches and pains
mysteriously arising within me morning before light.
Death sets up his reminders there, pain in my feet today,
yesterday my hands, the day before my head. What next?
I'll live with it. We're only here in borrowed flesh a little time.

DIPTYCH

I: Born Blind

The man had never seen the kind of light
you and I take for granted. Look, it's in my hands
this morning as I set out, stigmata bright,
my walk nothing short of the miraculous,
the sky paying respect to every branch and leaf.
Were I less naked to myself, each step
exposing my flesh to radiance, I might look back
to days I waited for clay to wash my eyes.
Five years back I was touched
by the unasked for, having given up on prayer.
Now all my mornings belong to a beginning seen again
as the blind man saw those hands across his eyes.
They were not hands. They were Christ releasing the
        first light,
the world seen, imperishable as it was to Adam
naked: stars, sun, moon. Today, a tree, a mockingbird,
the very ground under my feet immortal
before I give it names, then name it, twice-immortal
before I give it names and we begin to share our dying.

II: Release, Release

That day when I let go of everything—
it's out of sight, indescribable
in mortal words. That's why I have these poems.
Both you and I know all the words are God's.
I am the instrument, they play through me.
I say: the tree is forming in the sky.
Some call it Winter; I can name it Spring.
This poem needs green fecundity to speak.

All my trees' dead branches fill with unnamed birds.
Each is a music I will have to name
now as my body leaves me, first my feet
cold, then my knees, my cock, chest, throat and eyes.
I am Winter, turning, while I speak, to Spring.
Peter, let go. Now you have everything.

EMMAUS MORNINGS

Sometimes, in autumn, there comes that perfect day
midway to winter, when the world stands still,
every leaf as I approach it, turned to me.
I am going nowhere in particular,
just down the street to walk with the miraculous,
neither of us in the blue dark exactly awake yet.
These leaves: here in the Gulf South they are not
the luscious palette I would have them. But no matter.
Green has its permutations, too, in radiance
seen though the vision of the One who walks beside me,
my eyes His, these mornings of Emmaus on my street.
Lord, You are here most when I seek least.
How calm I am, now after years of prayer,
nights my lifelines were lifted to You, my desperate hours.

FIRST LIGHT MEDITATION

Beethoven in his deafness, the great sea
awakening in him, high tides breaking up
the shore, and then a new horizon standing there
when he stares: sea and sky meet, seamless.

Dickinson in her room: the afternoon
snow against her window, pain discs of snow
and diadems and doges surrendering.
She lifts the glass: Weather, my blood, come in.

Namesake, Peter, I must include you now?
You were no hero like the other two
but took, like me, multiple instances
to accept the divine made new each day
we open ourselves. So for you, for me,
there had to be a cock crowing three times
and then my tears, waiting years to appear,
took bodily form as sound, metaphor.
I found, still find, I can cry each morning
I go out to find the sun beside me,
companion not yet risen at world's end
to sun's new body as I'll rise to mine.
It's just light, the light of the world.
And I'm just my own Peter, taking it all down.

ALL MY TESTS NEGATIVE

Lepers who appear to Christ, appear to me
scabrous and multitudinous, eunuchs in chariots,
prostitutes naked in sin, you, the deaf and blind,
I need a miracle before I sleep tonight!
This is what I get: high noon, grace the light
standing between parked cars, the hospital parking lot,
all my tests negative, here between the black limo
trussed up to impress in milky leathers
mellifluous to the asses of the rich squeaking across them
and the pick-up stalled, hot wiring its only hope.
I am an American man on earth, ramrodding facts,
given to transcendence in quick, impatient thrusts.
The pick-up is a Ford, a kid is fiddling with it.
He's a pimply kid, thank God he's good at this.

THE ANNUNCIATION

From Everlasting all this came to pass.
Now, Christ come and gone, the world merely transformed,
you and I continuing the muddle of our days,
imagine with me how dark the sky those years
when all the prophets' words looked toward this birth.
The sky was not this morning's bluest blue.
If only I could find my image for that blue,
this language all reducible to miracle.
Instead, my poor syllables retell what you know.
A simple girl, she thought the angel was a bird,
and turning to it, violated by the words announced,
questioned at first her own virginity.
Then she saw it: my sky, your sky.
And so she put on the sun, the stars, the moon
and all the planets and wore them for herself,
a fourteen-year-old, crowned and terrified.

Three

"Brightness falls from the air."
—Thomas Nashe

NAMING-THE-ANIMALS-MOMENTS

The Audubon Zoo in New Orleans is hushed near closing time at 5:00 p.m. A few lost tourists wander by, here at the southwest extremity where I stand, staring down into the tapir pool.

The tapirs are not out. The tapirs are rarely out. Part of tapir-watching is the thrill of catching sight of an animal so shy it rarely shares the public spectacle of the other beasts.

I am looking for my mother who died two weeks ago at ninety-three-and-a-half. I have sought her because she is now memory and memory begins soon after a loved one's death to rewrite the past into touchstone moments. This waiting, both hands gripping the guardrail, is one such moment.

Growing up in the city of Detroit in the aftermath of World War II, I shared the zoo with Mother each summer. All little children love animals, I've discovered as father to two girls and a boy, but in most kids the fascination is replaced by others—ballet, gymnastics, art, cross-country, tennis, soccer. I had some of these interests later. But until age ten, the Detroit Zoo was my obsession, and I nagged my mother, who had a house full of relatives to care for when I was growing up, to take me there two or three times a week. There was a guardrail at the Detroit Zoo tapir pool, too. I am touching it now, standing here.

The light is falling at 4:30 p.m., the radiant New Orleans light I sometimes feel drew me down here from the Midwest and would keep me here even if I were not bound by the obligations of my teaching job. The light here is mystical, a nimbus around objects; it draws out some glow within them. Nothing is being drawn out of the tapir pool but memory.

My hand is in my mother's hand. We're in the tunnel at the Detroit Zoo; it's cool and dark. Mother squeezes my hand. I have put my hand into hers because I'm scared. Mothers are our first protection from the world; fathers protect us later. And this

afternoon the lunging of the miniature train, the squawk and whine
as we round corners invisible in the dark, sends shivers of excitement
and fear through my arms and legs, and hollows out the insides of my
mouth. My mother doesn't speak either. This is a moment winding
through time in its own tunnel and I'm all touch.

Suddenly gold light appears on the tunnel's walls and we're
racing faster toward it, then bursting forth into the sticky July day. I let
go of my mother's hand.

My hands continue to grip the New Orleans railing. The wood
is a little splintery as is the railing my little hands grasp to descend
from the zoo train with Mother. Now I am jumping off, scampering a
few steps from her, daring my mother to shout after me since she is a
protective mother. But she does not shout; she crosses to me in several
rapid steps and grabs my hand again. I cannot hear what she says
from this distance in time.

My mother is a good mother. We are living in the era of the
polio scare, an epidemic so rampant that even now, just as I am
learning to spell out words, the newspapers' headlines announcing
the death of another infant in Detroit, the bold black print, graced
sometimes with exclamation marks and a photograph of a child in an
iron lung, keep me on edge. Often, I will awaken at night in the black
stupor of our unairconditioned house, listening to the push of my
breath against my chest.

My mother's hand in mine is meant to rescue me from all sorts
of polio germs said to flourish in the world surrounding children at this
time. It is only because she cares about me, my mother repeats, that she
will take me to the zoo in the face of the polio epidemic. And it is only
if I *mind* that I am permitted to go at all.

Gripping my hand, my mother leads me away from the train.
All at once I am thirsty. Just before us, in an oasis of cool, surrounded
by a cluster of children, is a drinking fountain. I know already the

trials which await on my pursuit of this ambrosial liquid. I have been through this before.

If I *mind*, my mother will assure me, and *not for a second touch* the handle of the drinking fountain, she will let me have a drink. She has her procedure: with a hand wrapped in a handkerchief scented sweetly with a perfume, which always makes me think of light purple, she will touch the handle and turn it for me, lifting me across the belly to hover above the fountain. I must not touch my tongue to the nozzle, lest the contagion approach me and, as always, I nod dutifully.

We queue up, and all at once I am above the gold basin where water erupts from a two-pronged spray to splash wildly over the sides in an abundance of potential contagion if I do not *mind*, keeping my mouth dancing above the spray. How delicious this moment is, my mouth, so hollow within the tunnel, now aching with the cold water mine at last. No liquid since has ever tasted so quenching. How I wish, I think, I could float above the silver spray forever, staring down at my reflection in the gold basin. But there are other kids in line, many of them loose from their mothers. Now my mother is lifting me down, down from the magical water, onto the hot asphalt and again I feel her take my hand.

Now she releases it since our primary undertaking, so long delayed, must begin. For this, as always, I am to be the leader, she the follower. I may pick the animals we will give names to this afternoon. Of course, the tapir must be held back until later, for last if possible. Our visit to it will depend on the feeding times of the other animals.

The Detroit Zoo is one of the first zoos in the United States to put animals on islands surrounded by moats rather than in cages. Few animals, except an ancient lion and rare birds in the Bird House, are separated from us by the prisons which enclose their brothers in other habitats. To one of small stature, there is the thrill of looking directly across a moat you can choose to ignore, into the eyes of a tiger or hippopotamus. Such moments can be spellbinding, as on one trip from that garland of summers when I found myself face-to-face with a panda so docile of eye he could have been my cuddly companion for bedtime at home. The next moment he stood up on his hind legs, further confirming his role as toy, then bared a set of pink gums from which yellow teeth zig-zagged.

Oh, the names of the animals! They were real names; they were made-up names. They were all mine. A ring-tailed monkey I proclaimed "Jo-Jo," doubling the name of my best friend who had moved away; an elephant I renamed "Raja" instead of "Bill," the name the zoo had given him. A tortoise I baptized "Hortense," God knows why, or where I had heard the name, but when I first announced it to my mother she burst into laughter and swore I was an "unusual child." All mothers say that, don't they, when confounded by their sons?

There were other names, monosyllabic and polysyllabic, nicknames and brand names. Some animals I named for cars, such as the chimpanzee monikered "Deville," after my mother's powder blue Cadillac. Fat names, thin names, names delicious like the vanilla ice cream of childhood dripping from cones onto your hand, or freak names like "Waneenan" for an anteater, a creature so strange he perplexes me even today, names made of sugar and syrup so sweet they hurt your teeth repeating them, names which opened on vast plains, "Dakota" or "Nebraska" I had seen on our tiny black and white TV my father insisted be kept in the infrequently used dining room since TV, he announced, was a fad which wouldn't last.

To all of my choices my mother lent her approval, laughing or nodding as I ran ahead with my latest addition to this menagerie of nomenclature.

52

The choice animal, to be saved for last if possible, was the tapir. My fascination with this beast is inexplicable: maybe his sheer ugliness? The fact he looks like a combination of deer and pig? Whatever, the tapir was my favorite and though there were, according to the guidebook, five tapirs in the Detroit Zoo, they never appeared except as solo performers and were thus referred to by mother and me as "The Tapir."

Walking toward this creature who, as in the New Orleans Zoo, occupied the zoo's nether reaches, was in itself a special experience, to be protracted if possible. It was always up for grabs if his royal highness would make an appearance at all. In my memory today, however, the tapir is visible on his little island as we approach. My mother, though her interest in the animal is something only to be shared by me, expects me to look back at her—I do—and she returns my smile of delight. Together, we approach to bask in the glory of the thing-I-am-afraid-to-name.

The tapir meets our stare and moves off to redescend into the pool. The tapir moment is done. But it has been enough. I will go home now to construct my own zoo on the floor of my bedroom until dinner time, the tapir in a cage which I constructed out of fences I borrowed from my Lone Ranger Ranch, in the center of all.

And as I stand here in New Orleans, I see a tapir emerging from the black waters before me. Why he is making an appearance today I do not know. I am not necromancer enough to bring him forth. How very peculiar he is, I think again, an amalgam of beasts slowly emerging from unknown depths. Only a supernatural power could have conceived of him.

My hands still rest on the rail as I hear the groundskeeper calling out the closing hour. In Detroit, my mother would have insisted we start home long before this, as she had a 1940's dinner to prepare for half a dozen people. But I can let go of the guardrail now and allow the tapir to descend to his tapir-evening, tapir-night. My mother has brought him forth. She has been with me a solid hour during this visit to the zoo and that is long enough for even a good son to spend with his dead mother now. The presence of my mother is gone as I turn away from the tapir pool. She has left without saying goodbye or sharing some words of wisdom as she should if this were a parent-child object lesson.

I know my animal naming was the beginning of my first poems uttered before written down, poems conceived out of the desire to fix language of my own on creatures of the world I loved. To order, with music and color, my way. But this is no *Portrait of the Poet*. It's just a memory of my mother, missing from me again now as the afternoon's gold light soon will be, an afternoon among afternoons, a string of moments I carry with me.

Four

"I find ecstasy in living; the mere sense of living is joy enough."
— Emily Dickinson

PROEM

This morning: terror of the white page!
Terror of being happy in happiness!
Sparrows in my street, bent to some infinitesimal
crumbs or detritus I can't make out,
you wouldn't waste a sunrise on my little spinnings in myself,
now would you? When I am up and in the spirit
everything I touch is mine and can become a word
if I will listen. Bird at my window, trapped
the other side of glass, you are the word I would bring in.
The glass will not break. Hurl yourself against it,
scratch the cracked music of your beak and wings
against the pane. This I will transcribe, throwing in my touch of things—
the oven's flame, my deepening saffron tea, this pencil shaking syllables,
the salty pockets of my awakening body.
I will give myself this hour when I am God.

PROEM TWO: ALMOST POSTHUMOUS
POEM

Black window dawn, I turn to you again.
Teach me this morning how to write one star
across your morning so my name appears
there with the others, light beside the light.
Dawn, you know I'm not talking about fame,
whatever that is, only about us—
you, window, light and me, the elements
out of which spirit soars—and here it is.
Embarrassing to say this? God appears.
Yes, that's what happens, look, here on this page:
miracles write themselves, miracles, poems.

PROEM THREE: ALL MY POEMS ARE AUBADES

Or are they elegies?
Soulmaster, you I give the name of Peter
so I can talk to me, what is morning but a mourning,
grief but a celebration we awake alone.
And how weary, Lord, you must be of my bad poetry
dawn starts me writing as the blue dark lifts its lid
spilling the contents, gold and silver, indigo and red,
a treasure trove of color signifying nothing
until I find equivalents inside myself.
Back to the subject of the poem: what is it?
My dead, mother, sister and father who left me
last year, you're tired of me, too, aren't you?

AZALEAS
— for Tim Trapolin

God of this world, the only one I know,
this morning you have wakened me again,
terrified to witness so much beauty.

First light: my yard swells with their rioting:
there is nowhere I look I am not seen
by blossoms the sky opened while I slept.
Pink fills my eyes, I am alone with fire
such as the stars must walk through every night.

Therefore, I'm driven out to walk the streets,
forsaking my sleeping wife and children,
to see flowers pillage mansions of the rich
on the grand boulevards, drooping their blooms
on matron and maid, startled by pink light
or hours later find them still waking
clapboard houses of the working poor,
the poor drawn closer to the lushest blooms
I will not see this morning, hurrying,
I will not take the time to see ever
except when poems remember in minutes.

Now I have returned home I can say nothing.
I shave and shower and dress, assume the day,
no one to myself but a new man, changed
against my will by fallen stars, alive
again and again remembering light,
asking myself why I have been chosen
to have my eyes burned open by your grace.

TO MY MOTHER AND FATHER

You lived too long. I see that now.
Only to be keepers of my demonic sister
were you sustained the final years.
My visits to the home circled like your wheelchairs
turning about the dining room. Mother:
Why are we here? Dad: *Because we're here.*
Both of you sounding like a Gertrude Stein poem
you'd never read. Forty years back
the fortune teller on Coney Island, stretching out my hand,
told me my lifeline was very long. God, how long?

On my good days I awake to live forever,
child of the night, the light still not up yet.
Darkness, you too are my friend.
Nights, I put my palms up across your cold, starry face.
Let me receive the stigmata of moonlight
if that is all the grace light possible
to sustain me.
                How long, how many more mornings
will I run down my street, that light in my hands
promising all is possible? Wherever you are,
Sustainer, whatever you hear, how many more years
will I have, like this one released to night,
to morning, the place between,
released by doctors yesterday to perfect health?

THE WATCHERS

Being born again, blue morning hesitates
outside my window, it prefers the dark.
So do those night has yet to put to bed:
the man who has been up, looking for it.
High on his own words, he cries himself home:
I didn't get it, didn't get a thing.
The woman who has turned from trick to trick;
she scurries, she'd like cocoa, her own sheets.
The countless ones, whose house is on the stones
city fathers laid, some sleep, others watch
that sleepers not be robbed. Of what, I ask?

But God, who writes these poems, shakes His head,
smiles. How little you grasp, all the years
I've given you. You're like this stalling dawn,
darkness trying to keep light back from the sky
but always failing, and still you like success,
don't you? You know the day will always come,
but for these little ones a special night
is given. Witness how they don't complain.
They sleep in shifts. Try doing this for your wife,
your children. They share blankets. Try tonight
to stay awake all night so they can sleep.

THE ONE CERTAIN THING

A day will come I'll watch you reading this.
I'll look up from these words I'm writing now—
this line I'm standing on, I'll be right here,
alive again. I'll breathe on you this breath.
Touch this word now, that one. Warm, isn't it?

You are the person come to clean my room;
you are whichever of my three children
opens the drawer here where this poem will go
in a few minutes when I've had my say.

These are the words from immortality.
No one stands between us now except Death:
I enter it entirely writing this.
I have to tell you I am not alone.
Watching you read, Eternity's with me.
We like to watch you read. Read us again.

ADAM NAMING

At world's beginning there was poetry.
God said, "Let there be light." And there was light.
Sometimes I wish that those could be my poems—
days before He made us in his image
male and female, fruitful, multiplying—
I guess this puts me in God's first four days?

Oh, firmament-world that He called heaven,
my world down here is too much like your own.
How lonely I am with no companions.
Lights mark the seasons and the days and years,
the multiplying of great whales, living creatures.
All too perfect, my abundant place—
"and every winged fowl after his kind."
I am out of time, become a child,
my words playthings I move back and forth.
I could be in my room, back in Detroit,
lonely Peter, playing cars and trucks alone.

Reader, I'm moving on. Are you with me?
There's a whole world out there of poetry.
First there is Eden, Eve and nakedness,
the snake, the tree, but back of that
what I call " moments words become the flesh."
I mean the Adam-naming of it all,
cattle, fowl of the air, beasts of the field,
whatsoever I can name them now they are.

AFTERWORDS

How eager after my parents' deaths
I was to fly them home with me,
cummerbunds of Dad's I swore I'd wear,
Mother's gangrened European jewelry I hung on my wife.
I was practicing immortality, its artifice,
busying myself like a good shopkeeper those first months
inventorying my stuff: all the rooms of our small house
draped or arranged around my sacred relics.
Was it shop, museum or church I was reconstructing?
A golden bowl that could have been James' inspiration
waited on edge for my son's dribble or drop-kick
and a kitsch Greek head from the '30s sneered at me
in my study, announcing poetry could not be written
by a boy as little as the one I was making up
to wander a strange house, searching for his childhood.

I thought when I scavenged their apartment
discarding rusted shoe trees, corsets, three-cent stamps,
I was disposing of the past. That was the first act
in the three-part drama of the Afterdeath.
Part Two is trying on my father's ties,
broad as the tales I was fed of my family's normalcy
in our '50s house; it is stacking ashtrays
from Niagara Falls, Louis something-or-other from France,
another from a Packard dealer (*Ask the man who owns one* on the back)
in the closet since I'm trying to quit smoking
like I'm trying to quit gutting the past
with clutter, when it should be free to be Part Three, memory,
some good, some bad, most ordinary
like my father's giant hand lifting me on his back, Tom Thumb

for a ride or my mother flicking on a blue nightlight
since even today I am afraid to look into the dark
and see how little of me there is to fill the world
then or now, how empty of all of us the world longs to be.

MUSEUM OF THE MOMENT

Eight years dead now, my parents still come back
before the light, morning after morning.
Look, here they are: dressed for their honeymoon,
Dad in his porkpie, Mother in her cloche
caught by the flash just as the ship departs.
They stare at me from this photograph,
they tell me it is better to be dead.
Pete—the name they called me—we are happy.
This was our beginning, before the world
laid on us the burden of your sister,
her madness, abuse of you, your illnesses,
headaches and stomach pains and therapies.
Leave us in peace, you will have your moment
to choose the day you live eternally.

What about me? Well, what about you,
Mother answers, freshening her lipstick,
you have your life, leave us this afterlife.
Our ship leaves for Bermuda in an hour.
How do I look? I think this hat's smashing.
Two kids from Detroit; we were twenty-three.
Now I remember what's going to happen next—
invited tonight, is it my red hat?
(But Mother, our trips to the Detroit Zoo,
you hold my hand, we stare at the tapir . . .
Remember?) Yes, Dear, it doesn't matter.
To live forever, pre-crash '29,
to sit, dressed up, at the Captain's table!

THE LEAVES; THE ANIMALS; THE SKY UNSEEN

It's just this: everything will outlast us.
Our singularity? Temporary.
Peter's uniqueness is the end of him
like changing leaves my daughter mailed to me
from up North that I remember autumn
as New Orleans heats up for November—
their increase, dying, returning to the earth,
one leaf become another in its shades.
As if they knew, all the animals move
fluidly, trading their shadows today,
the zoo's feeding hour: lion, lioness
one being in their hunger, suspension
in time the only touch they have with death.

The leaves, the animals, the sky unseen
in cloud cover, then seen, remade, again
seconds later—how I will miss the world
when it insists I leave! I think I'll die
very quickly that they won't grieve too much,
the lions disappearing in their cages,
the end of day, zoo days, the end of days.

TO THE MORNING TREES

I

When I leave earth, I will miss you the most.
Always up before me, always upright,
standing above me with preparations for the day
ahead, you are my father multiplied, I knew at three.
Mornings I awake to assume that child.
He ages decades in seconds without prayer.

II

In school, I learned my life depends on you,
drawn breath by drawn breath. Oh, but I knew it,
the birds had taught me before I could speak
in human tongue and so could sing in theirs,
appearing at the window by my crib
that we warble to each other.

III

                    Departure,
my subject, I have been leaving earth since birth.
Sing with me, trees, wind running through your limbs,
when I run out this morning, arms uplifted,
the first day of my life, the best, the last,
a day I lift my slow hello to in my passing.

CORRESPONDENCES

Mornings before light in this beach house on the Gulf
my parents willed me, my grief not even one year old,
I wake to the waves' music: without asking they come back,
the ancient give-and-take I walked beside last night
too full of myself to find my rhythms in its own.
But this morning from my bed the waters forgive everything.
Unseen, they promise a new day to walk to
and duties thereof: beg the Salvation Army to return
for another truckload of the past I'm giving up.
First light exposes all these rooms as a sad tomb
such as the pharaohs left: I would if I could, display everything
for some museum I would meander, my parents resurrected
in stuff. I can't do that. I'll keep this silver napkin ring.
Dumb as it is, a gold bowl we gave them for fifty years together.

Undertow, swell and calm: I'll take my directions from your
        music as I go.

TO A DEPARTED SAVIOR

There are mornings I have awakened to live forever,
my body singing and the light arising with me.
I was a symphony of one sound, a color wheel
bursting with hues, the air stained glass ascending.
October: today I will murder my chrysanthemums
planting them too late. Still, each is essential—ochre, purple, rust.
Those black stalks, chill-bitten, could sustain me Christmas.

Savior, the prophets swear you will come back this century.
Could it be this Christmas Eve? Eight years ago near midnight,
my father died. Might he accompany you, the Second Coming?

Oh, Christ, today you are the one-eyed homeless man
hobbling the highway, raving, where I jog before I plant.
Who will have the guts to help you? Not me, hands in the cold
        ground.
Who will give me back my father, mornings of immortality?